THE ULTIMATE BEGINNER SERIES

BLUES BASS BASICS

STEPS ONE & TWO COMBINED

BY ROSCOE BECK

Additional Text by: Hemme Luttjeboer

Project Manager: Aaron Stang
Editor: Hemme Luttjeboer
Cover Layout: Joann Carrera
Technical Editor: Glyn Dryhurst
Engraver: Charylu Roberts

CONTENTS

Introduction

Welcome to the *Blues Bass Basics*. The following pages will guide you through the necessary requisites to playing and mastering blues bass guitar. A life-long study of classic bass lines by artists such as Muddy Waters, Elmore James, Howlin' Wolf, Albert King and B.B. King, etc., would be the ultimate approach, but this book will supply you with enough material to sound and play like the greats.

A basic knowledge of how to play the bass guitar is a pre-requisite, as well as some knowledge of music theory and elementary music reading capabilities. However beneficial, it is not necessary to be able to read music as all the examples are also written with tablature.

Topics like shuffles, slow blues, minor blues and two-beat feels are covered, as well as an examination of right and left hand techniques. On the CD, most of the examples are played slowly for initial presentation and then followed by actual playing settings with a trio consisting of bass guitar, electric guitar and drums for you to play along. Enjoy!

Section 1: The Basics

Tuning Methods

Tuning to a Keyboard

The bass guitar can be tuned to a keyboard. Match each of the four strings to the keyboard as indicated in the diagram. An electronic tuner is an alternative method to keeping your bass in perfect tune and for developing your ear to hear intonation accurately. However, if neither are available try to use the "5th fret" method below.

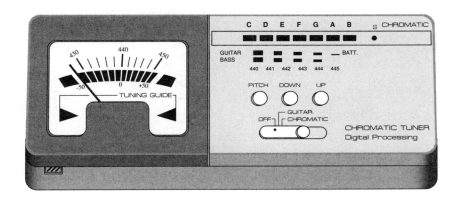

Tuning the Bass Guitar to Itself – The "Fifth Fret" Method:

1) Either assume your 4th string "E" is in tune or tune it to a piano or some other fixed pitch instrument.

2) Depress the 4th string at the 5th fret. Play it and you will hear the note "A," which is the same note as the 3rd string played open. Turn the 3rd string tuning key until the pitch of the open 3rd string (A) matches that of the 4th string/5th fret (also A).

3) Depress the 3rd string at the 5th fret. Play it and you will hear the note "D," which is the same as the 2nd string played open. Turn the 2nd string tuning key until the pitch of the open 2nd string (D) matches that of the 3rd string/5th fret (also D).

4) Depress the 2nd string at the 5th fret. Play it and you will hear the note "G," which is the same as the 1st string played open. Turn the 1st string tuning key until the pitch of the open 1st string (G) matches that of the 2nd string/5th fret (also G).

Musical Notation

Music is written on a staff. The staff consists of five lines and four spaces between the lines.

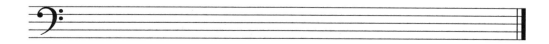

The names of the notes are the same as the first seven letters of the alphabet.

The notes are written in alphabetical order. The note on the first line is "G".

Notes can extend above and below the staff. When they do, ledger lines are added. Here is the approximate range of the bass guitar from the lowest note, open 4th string "E," to a "D," on the first string at the 17th fret.

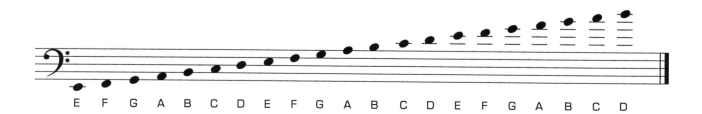

The staff is divided into measures by bar lines. A heavy double bar line marks the end of music. A dotted heavy double bar line signifies a repeat of a section of music.

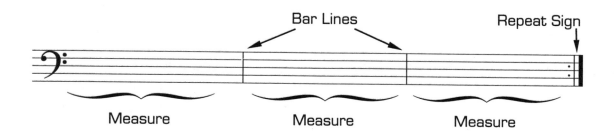

Tablature and Fretboard Diagrams

Tablature illustrates the location of notes on the neck of the bass guitar. This illustration relates the four strings of a bass to the four lines of tablature.

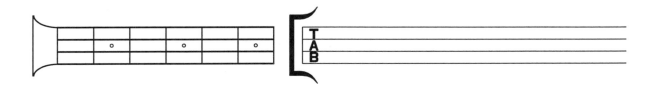

Notes are indicated by placing fret numbers on the strings. An "O" indicates an open string.

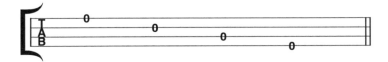

This tablature indicates to play the open, 1st and 3rd frets on the 4th string.

Tablature is usually used in conjunction with standard music notation. The rhythms and note names are indicated by the standard notation and the location of those notes on the bass guitar neck is indicated by the tablature.

Rhythm Notation and Time Signatures

At the beginning of every song is a time signature. 4/4 is the most common time signature:

4   FOUR COUNTS TO A MEASURE
4   A QUARTER NOTE RECEIVES ONE COUNT

The top number tells you how many counts per measure.
The bottom number tells you which kind of note receives one count.

The time value of a note is determined by three things:

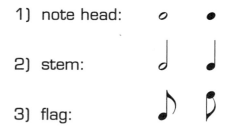

1) note head: o   ●

2) stem:

3) flag:

o   This is a whole note. The note head is open and has no stem. In 4/4 time a whole note receives 4 counts.

𝅗𝅥   This is a half note. It has an open note head and a stem. A half note receives 2 counts.

𝅘𝅥   This is a quarter note. It has a solid note head and a stem. A quarter note receives 1 count.

𝅘𝅥𝅮   This is an eighth note. It has a solid note head and a stem with a flag attached. An eighth note receives 1/2 count.

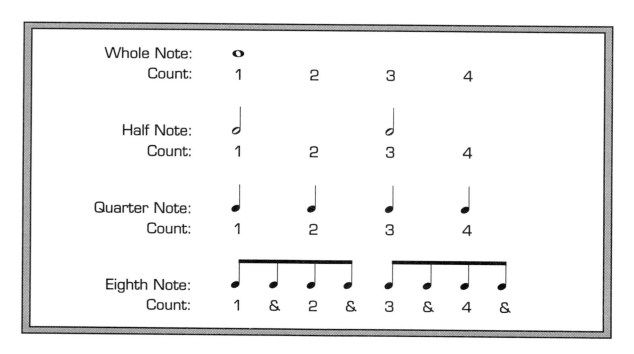

Whole Note:	o			
Count:	1	2	3	4
Half Note:	𝅗𝅥		𝅗𝅥	
Count:	1	2	3	4
Quarter Note:	𝅘𝅥	𝅘𝅥	𝅘𝅥	𝅘𝅥
Count:	1	2	3	4
Eighth Note:	𝅘𝅥𝅮 𝅘𝅥𝅮 𝅘𝅥𝅮 𝅘𝅥𝅮	𝅘𝅥𝅮 𝅘𝅥𝅮 𝅘𝅥𝅮 𝅘𝅥𝅮		
Count:	1 & 2 &	3 & 4 &		

Basic Theory and Definitions

Here is a brief compendium of fundamental harmony and scale theory that is referred to as it applies to the bass guitar. Whether a new topic or simply a refresher for you, this material is beneficial in understanding most of the text and examples used. A more in depth study would elaborate on each of the examples but the following will provide an elementary introduction to basic theory.

Interval: Distance between two notes, whether played together or in succession

Interval of a minor third: three semi-tones (frets)

Interval of a major third: four semi-tones (frets)

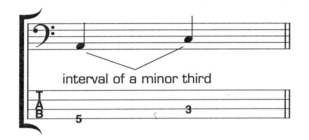

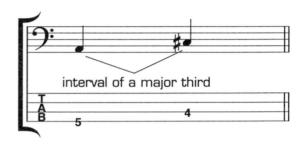

Chord: A combination of three or more different notes

Triad: A combination of three notes consisting of any note with the interval of a major or minor 3rd and a 5th above

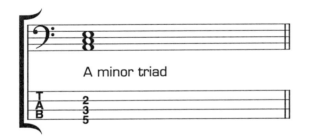

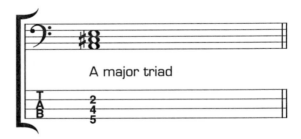

Arpeggio: A chord which is played melodically; notes sounding consecutively

Four part chord: A triad with a major 7th or ♭7th degree added

Am7 arpeggio

A7 arpeggio

Scale: A series of notes rising and/or falling, according to some system, usually encompassing an octave

Pentatonic scale: A five note scale

Major pentatonic scale: A five note scale containing root, second, third, fifth and sixth

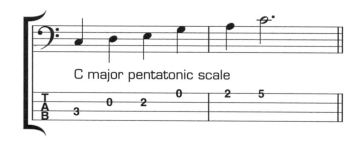

C major pentatonic scale

Minor pentatonic scale: Contains the same notes as the major pentatonic scale but starts on the 6th degree

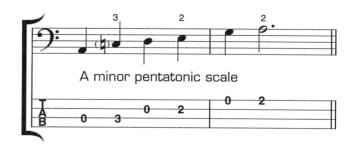

A minor pentatonic scale

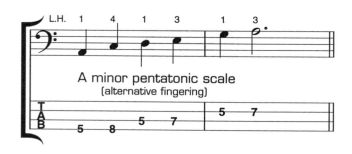

A minor pentatonic scale
(alternative fingering)

Blues scale: A minor pentatonic scale with a flatted 5th between the 4th and 5th degrees

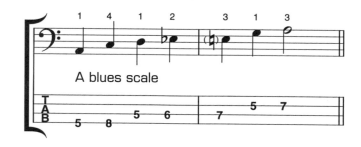

A blues scale

③ *Technique and Hand Positions*

Hold the bass so it feels as natural and comfortable as possible in sitting or standing position. The left hand should grasp the neck with the thumb freely pivoting behind the neck at the midway point. This will give your fingers freedom of motion as they curl around the neck. The fingertips should be held almost perpendicular to the frets *(see diagram)*. The right hand thumb floats on top of the 4th string, not anchored, and can be used as a mute for open or unused strings. Left hand fingerings have been included in most of the music examples to get you started but you are encouraged to experiment.

Equipment

Blues songs usually require a solid, full bass sound. Bass and guitar players can choose between a passive or an active instrument. An active instrument means that its pickups are powered by a battery whereas a passive does not require any. It is a matter of taste which type of bass you play as well as how you amplify your instrument. You can use a tube amplifier, pre-amp or a solid state amplifier to broadcast your groove but you will hear which type of equipment best meets or suits the authenticity of the blues.

You have a choice of round wound or unwound strings as well. Wound strings encompass a steel string core that is fully covered with a thin, tightly wrapped strand of nickel or equivalent metal. Unwound strings are not covered. String gauges vary but a typical set could comprise of a .045mm for a first (G string) to .105mm for a 4th string. After experimentation you will more than likely adhere to whatever plays and sounds the best for you. You may even include a "5 string" bass as part of your set up. The 5th string, a low "B," gives you an extended harmonic range and is very flexible and efficient for your position playing.

Section 2:
The 12-Bar Blues Progression

It is essential that you familiarize yourself with the 12-bar blues form. All the examples in this book are based on this form. The earliest rural blues relies on the basic **I-IV-V** chord progression. The chords are derived from the three primary triads of the major scale. However, the addition of the ♭7th degree to each chord adds to the tension and dominant blues quality of the progression. The basic blues form consists of four bars of the I chord, two bars of the IV chord, two bars of the I chord again, two bars of the V chord and finally two bars of the I chord (see below). This 12-bar succession of chords usually repeats itself over and over again enlisting the improvisational skills of the musicians.

A variation of this progression has been called the "quick change" blues progression. For more harmonic interest, the IV chord is introduced briefly in measure 2. Then return to the I chord. In the tenth bar, the IV chord is reinstated after the V chord before returning to the I chord in measure 11. In the final bar, measure 12, a "turnaround" is created by playing the V chord, which acts as a springboard and simply sets up the entire progression for repetition.

12-Bar Blues

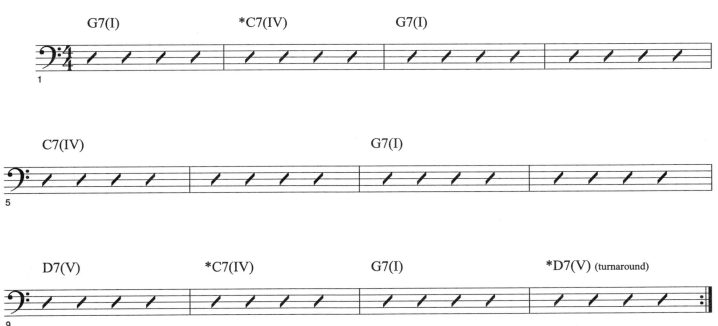

*These chords are used in the "quick change" blues progression.

CD
(5) ## Shuffle Blues Bass Lines

Most of the examples in this book are played in the "shuffle" or 12/8 feel. A shuffle feel is created from the triplet figure, (♪♪♪) three eighth notes played in the time it takes to play two eighth notes or a quarter note. The first two notes, however, are tied together (♪♪♪). Songs written with a shuffle feel will have a shuffle indication at the beginning. This means that although the eighth notes are written normally (♫) they are played in the triplet feel (♪♪).

CD
(6) ## Example 1: Roots and Triads

The first example is a shuffle that Elmore James popularized but Robert Johnson may have invented. The bass line reinforces the chord progression with simple quarter note roots on the I, IV and V chords for the first "chorus." (A chorus in the blues genre is one complete 12-bar cycle of the chord progression.)

The second chorus in this example is based on simple "triads" of each chord. (A major triad consists of the root, the major 3rd and the 5th of a chord.) For example, the foundation of the I chord "E" is: E (the root), G♯ (the major 3rd) and B (the 5th).

Chorus 2:

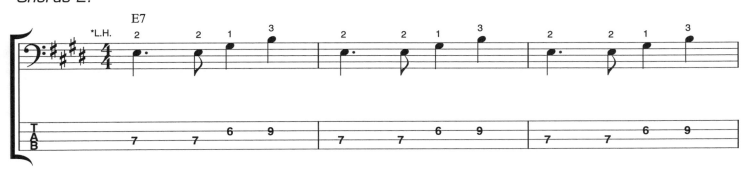

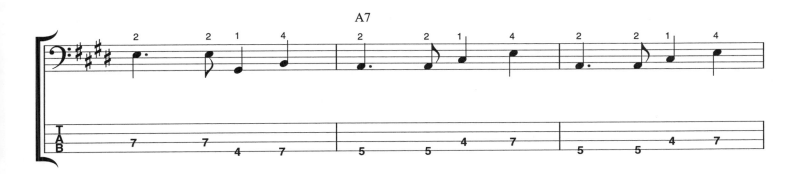

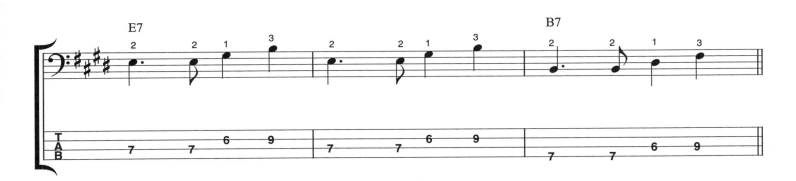

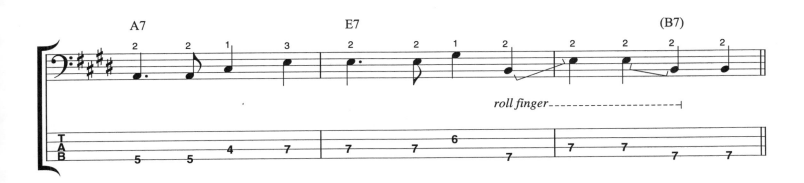

The third chorus is supported by "root/5th" activity in the bass using eighth notes. It returns to familiar territory with simple quarter note roots for the final chorus. Watch your left hand fingering when you play the third chorus; when playing two notes with the same finger, roll that finger from string to string, play both notes staccato (detached). Don't let them "ring" into each other.

Chorus 4:

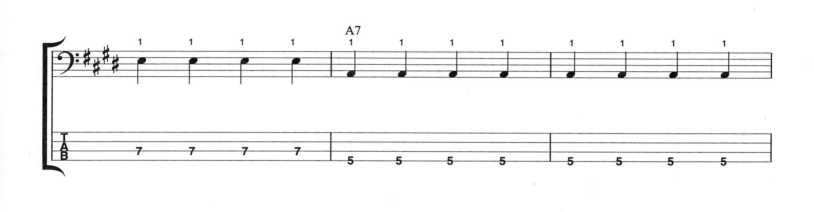

CD
(7) **Example 2: The 6th Degree**

This example is an extension of the triad idea; it introduces a fourth tone, the major sixth of the chord. For the G chord the sixth is "E," for the C chord the sixth is "A" and for the D chord the sixth is "B."

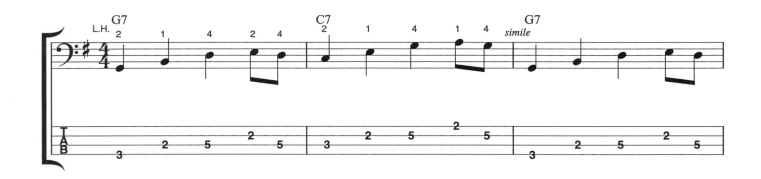

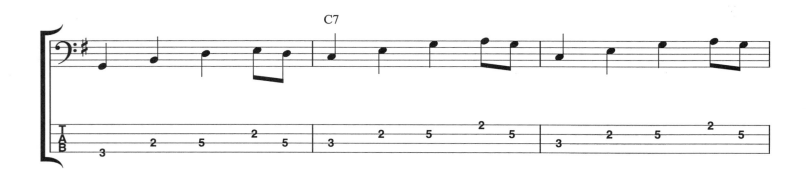

CD (8) ## *Example 3: Muted Notes*

Practice Example 3 and then play Example 4 with the band. Try this example as an alternative to Example 2. Instead of playing the second eighth note (the pickup to the downbeat) as a real note, fake or "mute" it. Do this by not actually fretting the note, instead lightly touch the string with your left hand. You can achieve this effect anywhere on the neck. Use it as an accent or "pickup" to propel the music along. In addition to adding to the feel of the tune, it facilitates your position shifts because you are not committed to playing the "actual" note before you make your hand shift.

*Muted note.

CD (9) ## *Example 4*

Example 5: Dropped Octave

Yet another variation of the triad with the added sixth tone is suggested in this line in the key of C. By dropping down an octave to the 5th of the chord (G) in the second and fourth measures, it reinforces the tonic (C) on the first beat. Listen to Example 5A and play with the band.

CD (10) **Example 5A**

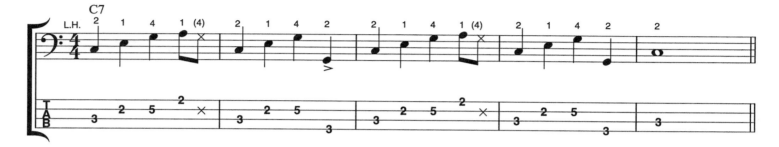

CD (11) **Example 5B**

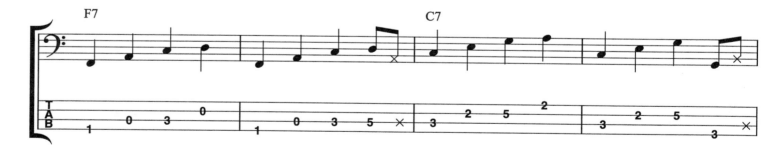

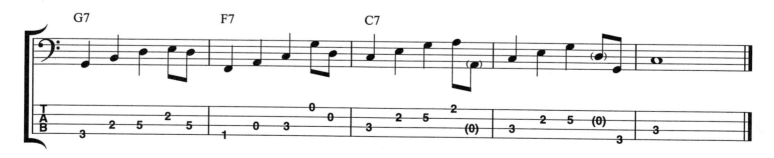

CD
⑫ *Example 6: Chromatic Passing Tone*

Here we have the introduction of non-chord and non-scale notes. The G♭ (F♯) is referred to as a "chromatic" passing tone and lies between the root (G) and the ♭7th (F) of the G7 chord. A chromatic note (C♯) bridges the 4th (C) and the 5th (D) as well. Note that each of these "passing tones" is an eighth note and does not appear on a strong beat ("1," "2," "3" or "4").

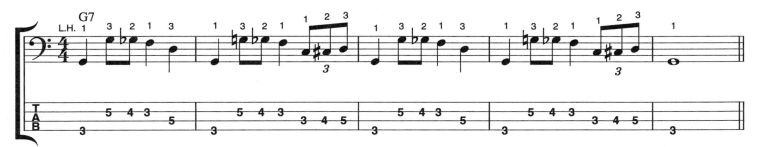

CD
⑬ *Example 7: Triplets*

Once you have the previous study under your fingertips, play along with the band in this example.

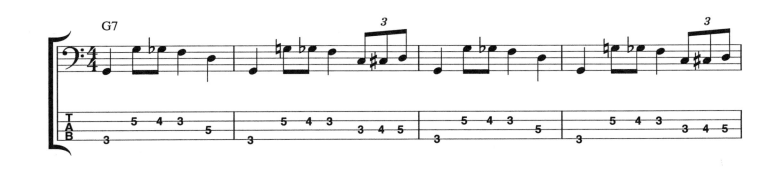

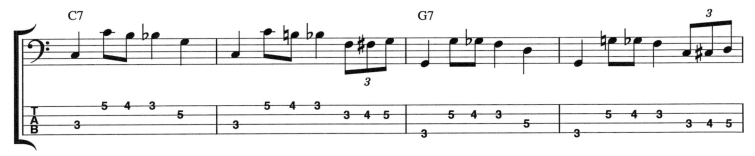

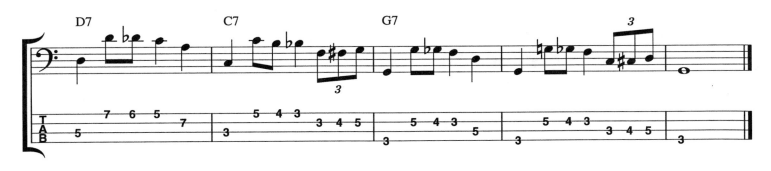

CD
(14) *Example 8*

Example 8 is simply a variation using triplets on every fourth beat.

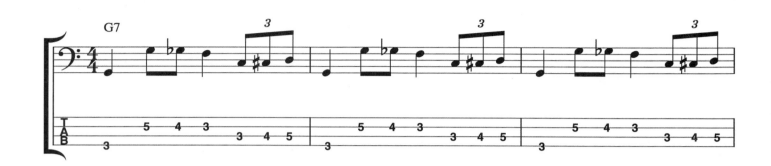

CD 15

Example 9: Memphis/Jimmy Reed Feel

This familiar line is referred to as the "Memphis" or "Jimmy Reed" feel. It is distinguishable by what the guitarist plays. Namely, in this example in the key of A, he plays A5, A6, A7 and back to A6 — two beats per chord. This bass line outlines an A7 chord over two bars with an accented octave, A, on the third beat. Transpose this hip idea to as many "blues" keys as you can.

Example 10: Open String Bass

Examples 10A and 10B are the same bass line, first in G and then in the key of E with open strings. Pay particular attention to muting the open strings so they don't ring on through the phrase.

CD 16

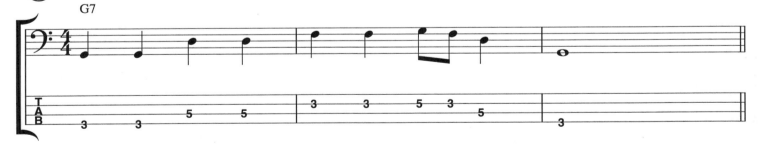

CD 17

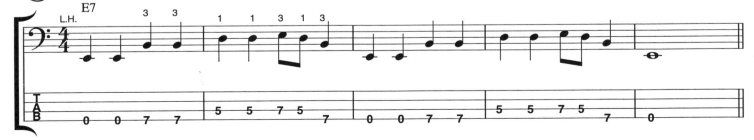

CD
(18) *Example 11: 2/2 or Cut Time*

Example 11 is your chance to use some of the bass lines covered so far with the band. The two choruses have been written in 2/2 or "cut time." This means that there are two strong beats to a measure. You could count quickly in common time (4/4) and simply refer to the snare drum as it strikes beats two and four while you tap your foot on beats one and three. This is why the form of the progression looks twice as long as we have been used to. It is somewhat of a precursor to the next topic.

A7

D7

A7

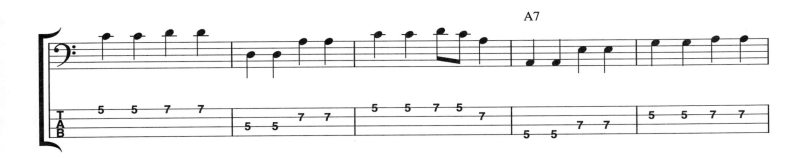

E7   D7

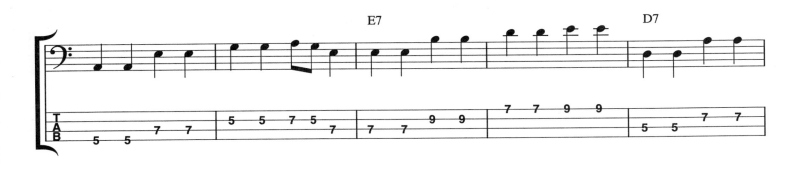

A7

CD 19 **Two Beat Blues Feel**

The "two beat blues feel" actually evokes a half time feel over common time measures. It can be heard as a "New Orleans style march feel". In the first measure of Example 12, half notes outline the chord with a simple root/five. But the second bar uses the sixth degree on the 4th beat to end the little "two bar" phrase.

CD 20 **Example 12: New Orleans Style March Feel**

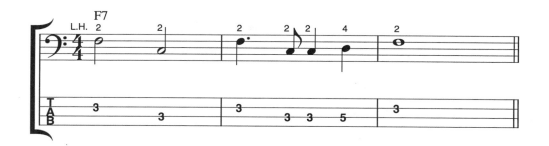

CD 21 **Example 13**

Here we use our "muted note" technique to enhance this little gem. On the "and" of beat three in the second bar, release the fretted note (C) just enough to get a muted sound before striking beat four.

This can be a very effective way of pushing the groove along. You should get the idea once you play through Example 14.

CD 22 **Example 14**

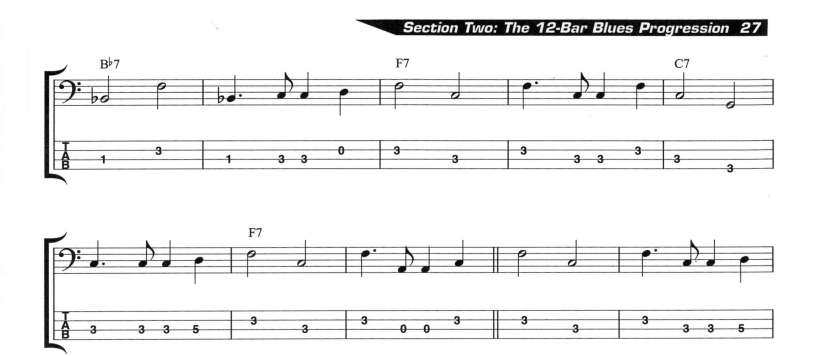

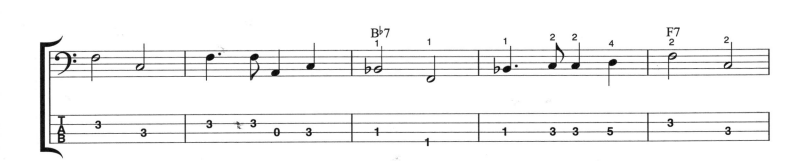

CD
(23)

Section 3: The Slow Blues

Probably the most familiar sound in all the blues is the "slow blues." The 12-bar patterns in this section are based on the dominant 7th (♭7th) chord. In the key of G, G is the root, B is the major 3rd, D is the 5th and F is the ♭7th. In the following examples, a few non-chord tones, which we referred to as "chromatics", are used as passing tones.

CD
(24) *Example 15: Using The ♭7th*

In Example 15, a G7 chord is outlined with a passing tone on the 4th beat inside a triplet. The triplet is the essence of the pulse of the "slow blues" and by playing it on the 4th beat emphasizes the groove.

Example 16: Using A Simple Triad

In Example 16A, a simple but effective triad lays claim to the bassline. But in Example 16B, a powerful triplet on the second beat covers the 3rd and 5th of G as it leads to the ♭7th, F.

CD
(25) **Example 16A**

CD
(26) **Example 16B: Triplets (12/8 feel)**

CD
(27) # Example 17: Walking The Bass

This next example involves a technique along the lines of how a jazz bass player would approach a standard blues. "Walking the bass" involves a combination of chord-scale and passing-tones played in quarter notes. Chromatic tones are usually resolved by a half step, meaning that they are only a semi-tone away from a strong scale or chord tone.

CD
(28) # Example 18

Listen carefully to the band in this example then play along. A very strong triplet feel dominates each of the five choruses. The last one is a composite of the preceding techniques. Notice the brief interaction in bar four (G7) by the drummer and bass.

Chorus 2:

Chorus 3:

CD 29

Section 4: Minor Blues

The minor blues is another very popular sound of the blues, especially with the slow 12/8 feel. The chords are still I-IV-V but are now minor instead of major. This simply means that all the I, IV and V chords are minor rather than major or dominant.

The minor blues can be played several different ways, often resembling a slow blues in a major key. The only difference is that the bass line in a minor blues often employs a minor 7th **arpeggio** (the notes of the related chord played one at a time in succession).

Example 19: Minor 7th Arpeggios

Example 19A is a bass line over A minor7 with a 12/8 feel and is a prelude to Example 19B. Notice that the bass simply arpeggiates the chord changes to each bar.

CD 30 **Example 19A**

CD 31 **Example 19B**

CD 32 ***Example 20: "Green Onions" Style***

This next example is a bass line with the same chords; Am7-Dm7-Em7. You may recognize it as the bass line from a tune called "Green Onions" by Booker T. and the M.G.'s as well as "Help Me" by Sonny Boy Williamson. This time the fourth degree is used momentarily as an eighth note on the first half of the fourth beat. In the previous examples where the bass line does not include the major or minor third degree but relies mainly on movement between the ♭7th, 5th and/or 4th degree, the line can work equally as well over a minor blues progression.

Example 21

Listen to Example 21. It is the same bass line as Example 8, the only difference between the two is in the chord harmony. The following is in a minor key.

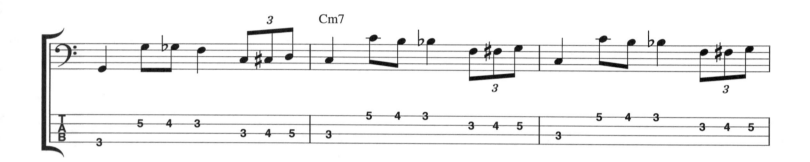

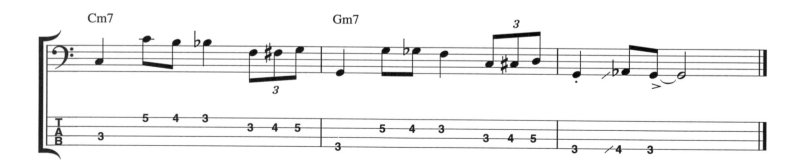

CD (34) ## *Example 22: Fever Style*

By staying in the 12/8 shuffle mode and in the key of A minor we play a two measure minor 7th line reminiscent of a tune called "Fever."

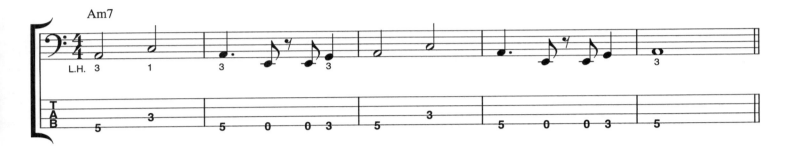

CD (35) ## *Example 23*

Play along with Example 23. It is a simple but very effective line.

CD **36** *Example 24: The Thrill Is Gone*

One of the most popular and enduring blues progressions of the last twenty-five years is "The Thrill Is Gone" by B.B. King. It is a 12-bar minor blues and a little different than any example so far. The difference arrives at the ninth and tenth measures. Instead of going to the minor V chord in bar nine, the resolution is delayed by the insertion of the major VI chord (G) followed by a dominant V7 chord (F♯7), which resolves back to the Im7 (Bm7). The bass line from this B.B. King classic outlines the root, 4th, 5th and ♭7th of each chord. Basic, but again extremely effective!

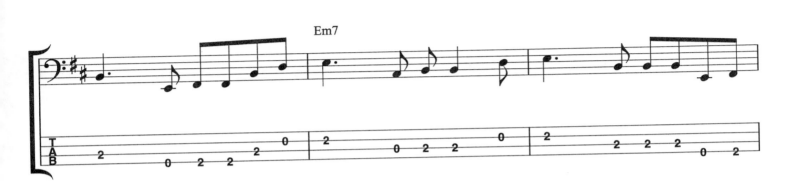

CD
(37)

Section 5: Alternative Styles

Like jazz music, the blues has absorbed other musical influences. For example, styles such as "rhythm and blues" evolved from early rural blues and in turn have influenced today's blues music. Latin music has even left it's signature on the blues. The following bass-line examples typify a few of those blues "grooves" that you may come across.

CD
(38)

Example 25: The Latin Surf

Example 25 can be described as a "Latin/surf" beat. The line spells out the root and the ♭7th of the chord, with the assistance of a chromatic push by the major 7th to the root. Because no major or minor third is present, the line can be played over a major or minor progression.

CD 39 *Example 26*

A similar line is shown in Example 26. Note that it contains ideas we have already learned from previous examples; the "muted" note on the second beat and the "chromatic passing tone" on the fourth beat. The line centers around the root, 5th and the ♭7th. This is inspired from a tune called "Born In Chicago" from the first Paul Butterfield Blues Band album.

CD 40 *Example 27*

Play along with this example to "feel the groove." Watch the last two measures in particular. The very last bar is played with a "band cue." This means that the ending or last note is played via a mutually agreed upon signal. It is usually accomplished with a simple nod or similar gesture.

CD ④① ## *Example 28: The Latin/Rhumba Feel*

This next example is a Latin/rhumba type feel using the root, major 3rd, 5th and 6th degree from the chord. This bass line is influenced by a tune called "Cross Cut Saw" by Albert King. The "syncopated" beats (the "and" of "2" and "3") draw out the Latin/rhumba feel. Again the bass guitar follows the standard blues progression in the key of Ab major.

CD ④② ## *Example 29*

Play Example 29 and memorize this line in different keys.

Example 30: Bo Diddly Style

Here is a bass line that is not very challenging harmonically but makes up for that deficiency in its rhythm. It is in the realm of guitarist "Bo Diddly" and adheres to the basic root, its octave and occasionally the ♭7th. It has a quasi-Latin ambiance to it and is propelled again with the "muted" note. This note is played on an open third string to create movement. Practice Example 30A a few times before playing Example 30B with the band. The example has been written here in 2/2 (cut time) to facilitate reading with simple quarter and eighth notes. The form looks twice as long as the usual 12-bar progression.

Example 31: '60s R&B/Soul

This example shows us the kind of effect '60s Rhythm and Blues and soul music has had on the blues. Stalwart bass players like James Jamerson and Chuck Rainey had an enormous impact on the music at that time and it is revealed in these syncopated lines. The two measure line falls nicely over each chord change except when we get to the ninth and tenth bars; here we have a different chord for each measure. So a little quick thinking will reveal that if you play the first half of the two-bar line on the V chord (E7) at bar nine, and then the second half of the line which you played over the IV (D) chord over measure ten, you will resolve nicely to the I (A7) chord at bar eleven. Whew! It is much easier to play than to read. So, run through this example a few times before playing with the band at Example 32.

Example 32

Section 6: Play Along

CD (47) *Example 33: "A7 Funk Jam"*

This is an open jam for you to explore the bass lines from Example 32. There are six choruses here with the ending written out. The actual bass guitar track you hear is intentionally ambiguous as it imitates a second electric guitar part and tries to stay clear of your playing.

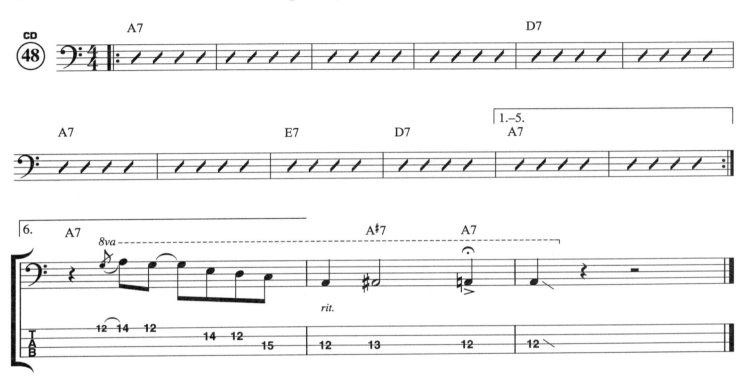

CD (49) *Example 34: "Shuffle Jam"*

This is a "shuffle" for you to try some more of the ideas presented in this book. Again the actual bass guitar on the track echoes a second electric guitar. There are seven choruses for you to ad lib. and create a solid bass line. Note the G minor "pentatonic scale" played by the bass guitar on the ending.

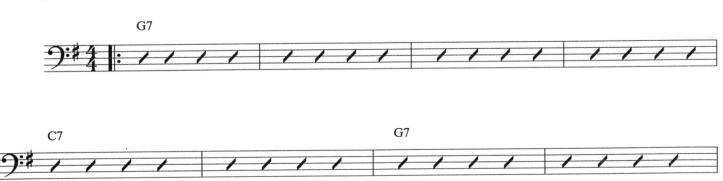

CD 50 **_Example 35: "Big Boss Man"_**

This number is played with additional support by keyboard and vocals. It is similar to "Big Boss Man," and it is a prime example of the "Memphis/Jimmy Reed feel" similar to Example 9. This one is in the key of E major and written in "cut time." You should be able to follow the bass player as he sticks close to a familiar line. There are four choruses with the ending included.

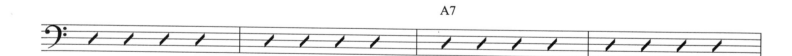

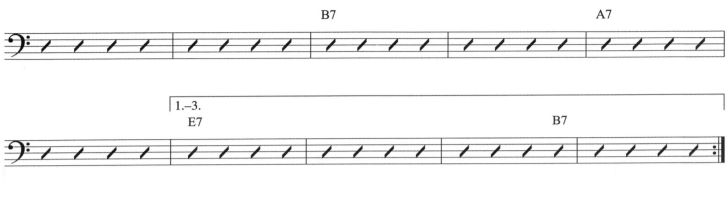

Example 36: "Help Me"

CD (51)

Here is an A minor blues similar to "Help Me" by Sonny Boy Williamson. It exemplifies the natural minor blues we covered earlier. Actually it is the same progression as Example 20. There are seven choruses for you to play along before it fades out.

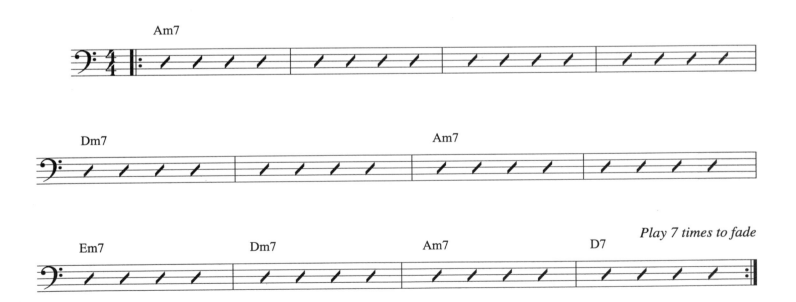

Play 7 times to fade

CD
(52) # Example 37: "Everyday I Have The Blues"

This jazz/blues example is similar to "Everyday I Have The Blues." We haven't explored this particular chord sequence in detail but the chord chart is easy to follow. The bass outlines the chords with the "walking bass" technique we studied previously. The chords in this chart are written with basic ♭7th chords even though the piano and guitar actually play extensions of the basic harmony. Listen extensively to the bass player as he uses solid quarter notes to walk through the nine choruses. The ending has been written out.

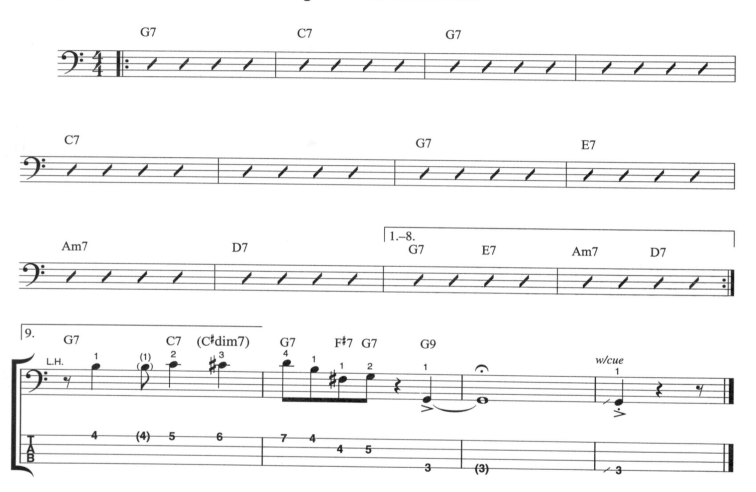

Closing

The key to really mastering the blues is to "get out there and play." Listen to recordings by the original blues artists that created the styles that we have covered as well as the blues players from the '40s, '50s and '60s. There is a wealth of information to be learned.

Play and "jam" with friends and/or put a band together. Try to find every opportunity you can to play your bass. For a more in depth view of blues bass, consider the video by Roscoe Beck called "Blues Foundations" on REH Video.